Starting School

Mary O'Keeffe

Name the things in the picture that begin with s.

Look, trace and say

This is a capital

S

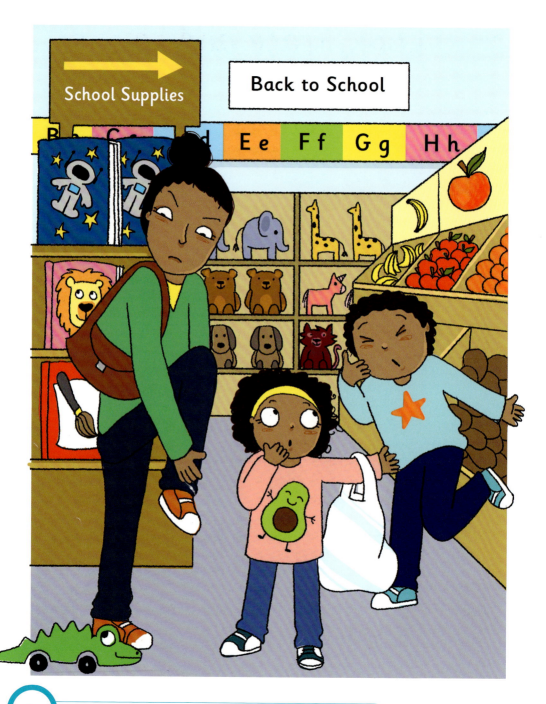

4 Name the things in the picture that begin with a.

Look, trace and say

This is a capital

A

Name the things in the picture that begin with t.

Look, trace and say

This is a capital

T

Name the things in the picture that begin with i.

Look, trace and say

This is a capital

I

10　Name the things in the picture that begin with p.

Look, trace and say

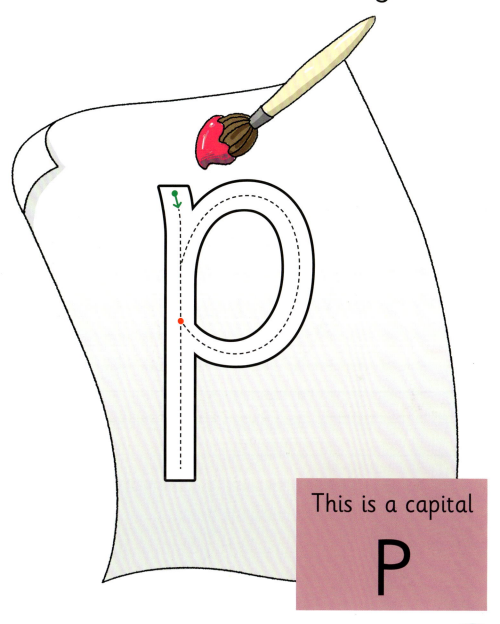

This is a capital

P

Name the things in the picture that begin with n.

Look, trace and say

This is a capital

N

Name the things in the picture that begin with c.

Look, trace and say

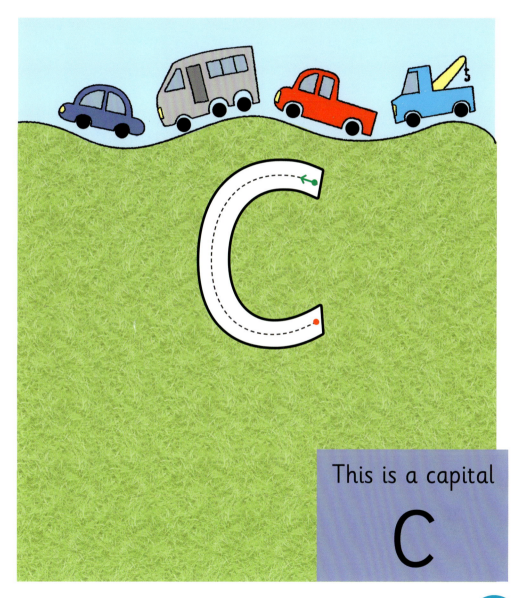

This is a capital

C

I can look, trace and say

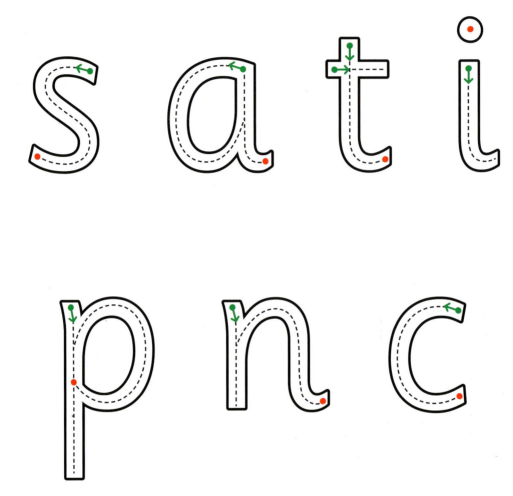